THE

Bernice Hurst

Illustrations
by Ronald Hurst

HAMLYN

Published 1985 by Hamlyn Publishing,
a division of The Hamlyn Publishing Group Ltd,
Bridge House, 69 London Road,
Twickenham, Middlesex

© Elvendon Press 1981, 1985

ISBN 0 600 32531 8

Printed in Italy

CONTENTS

INTRODUCTION

The word "pie" is used in reference to many dishes made with pastry – quiches, flans, tarts, pasties etc. It is a universal term, guaranteed to tempt the eye and the palate. But, although pastry is a basic item in cookery, and easy enough to make, it can also be an art form. Once the technique has been mastered, the way is clear for choosing from sweet, savoury, soft, crispy or flaky. The sky is the limit where decorations are concerned. Pies can truly be masterpieces. But first, of course, a few lessons must be learned.

Pastry should not be handled too much. Fat should be room temperature, not too cold (hard), not too warm (soft). Rubbing in should be done lightly, with the fingertips. This term refers to the method of combining fat and flour and means just what it says. The flour should be gently rubbed together with the fat until the mixture resembles fine breadcrumbs. Your pastry will come out particularly light if, during the rubbing in, you keep your hands well above the bowl and rub the mixture through your fingers rather than against them. Liquids should be bound in with a knife and kneading should be kept to a minimum. To ensure that bottom crusts are cooked thoroughly, the pie plate should be placed on a pre-heated baking tray. Sifting the flour first will make your pastry lighter. Chill pastry before using it for easy handling. When rolling, turn the pastry in quarter circles but do not flip it over. Instinct will tell – as with babies, be firm but gentle.

Many recipes suggest that pastry should be "baked blind". This is to make sure that your pastry is cooked before you add the filling to an open pie or tart. Line the pie dish, ensuring that the dough is pressed down well and no air remains. Then, either prick the dough with a fork or line it with tin foil and cover the base with rice or dried beans. This will prevent the pastry shrinking. If it does shrink, you will end up with a base, but no sides, or very uneven sides, rather than a nice neat case waiting to be filled. If you use tin foil, remove it after 10-15 minutes, when the pastry feels firm, to allow the pastry to brown. Place the pie dish on a pre-heated tray and bake 20 minutes at 200C/400F/gas 6.

Pastry freezes very well. It can be prepared in quantity and frozen in convenient size packs. Most pies freeze well. Double crusted pies can be frozen before they are baked. Open pies should be cooked first, then frozen.

There are two important categories of pie which have been omitted from this book. The first is those made with puff pastry, the second those made with hot water, or raised pastry. Puff pastry can be used to wrap virtually anything or as a base for whatever fillings you can think of. Recipes are not always necessary – just turn your imagination loose. Hot water pastry, on the other hand, requires very particular recipes, and here space did not permit. Neither type should be neglected, but a much larger volume would be necessary to do them justice.

Pies have always been popular. They can be the simplest things you cook or the most elaborate. Either way, a bit of care and thought will please your friends and family and can easily result in The Perfect Pie.

PASTRY

The pastry recipes given here should ensure that your repertoire is geared to any pie you choose to make. Pâte sucrée is light and crispy, but differs from shortcrust in that it is not flaky. The flavour and texture of shortcrust can be altered by using different proportions of fat. The sweet and egg pastries are both soft and need to be handled with care. All quantities given are sufficient to line a 23-cm/9-inch pie plate.

PÂTE SUCRÉE

175 g/6 oz flour	75 g/3 oz sugar
75 g/3 oz butter	3 egg yolks

Make a well in the centre of the flour and add the other ingredients. Using the tips of your fingers, lightly rub together the butter, sugar and egg yolks. Gently draw in the flour until a dough is formed. Wrap in cling film or a plastic bag and chill well before rolling. Pâte sucrée does not shrink when it is baked. It should be watched carefully during baking, however, as it can brown very quickly.

RICH EGG PASTRY

175 g/6 oz flour	2 egg yolks
75 g/3 oz margarine	1-2 tbsp iced water

Combine the egg yolks and water. Dice the margarine and rub into the flour until the mixture resembles fine crumbs. Stir in the egg and water with a knife until a dough is formed. Wrap and chill before rolling.

SHORTCRUST

175 g/6 oz flour	pinch salt
75 g/3 oz fat	1-3 tbsp water

Dice the fat into small pieces. Gently rub the fat into the salt and flour until it resembles fine crumbs. Stir the water in, 1 tbsp at a time, with a knife until a dough is formed. Wrap or cover with a clean cloth, and chill before rolling.

Depending on the sort of pie you plan to make, the fat can be half lard and half margarine, all lard or all butter for a very soft pastry. For a sweet pie, ground nuts can be substituted for part of the flour. Wholemeal flour can also be used, either on its own or mixed with white flour. For savoury pies, seasoning can be added or 25 g/1 oz of grated cheese stirred into the flour before making the dough.

SWEET PASTRY

175 g/6 oz flour	1 tbsp sugar
100 g/4 oz soft margarine	1-2 tbsp water

Combine the margarine, water and 3-4 tbsp flour. Gradually add the remaining flour and sugar. Mix well. Cover and chill before using. As this pastry is very soft, it is often necessary to press it into the pie dish rather than rolling it.

PASTIES

*Individual pies make excellent picnic fare, snacks or lunches.
They can be made in pie dishes if you have them, or the pastry
can be cut in circles and folded in half over the filling for the
traditional pasty shape.*

Meat Pasties

450 g/1 lb stewing steak	1 turnip, chopped
1 onion, chopped	(optional)
1-2 potatoes, chopped	salt and pepper
2 carrots, chopped	450 g/1 lb pastry

Sausage Pasties

450 g/1 lb sausage meat	1 tsp mixed herbs
2 potatoes, chopped	1 egg, beaten
1 onion, chopped	450 g/1 lb pastry

For meat pasties, cut the stewing steak into very thin slivers,
or dice into tiny cubes. For the sausage pasties, use the best
sausage meat available. Combine all the filling ingredients,
except the beaten egg which will be used for sealing and
glazing the pasties.

Roll out 450 g/1 lb of your favourite pastry – puff,
shortcrust or cold dough (see Sweeney's pies) are equally
good. Cut into circles and place a spoonful of filling on each.
Brush the edges with egg, seal well and brush again. Place
on a greased baking tray. Bake 40-50 minutes at 190C/375F/
gas 5. *Serves 4-6*

SWEENEY'S CHICKEN PIE

Sweeney & Todd is a pie shop in Reading, Berkshire owned by June and Alan Hayward, which produces some of the best pies we have ever sampled. The recipes they have shared with us are simple to follow, open to variation and produce beautiful results every time.

Half Puff Pastry

175 g/6 oz flour	50 g/2 oz margarine
25 g/1 oz lard	4½ tbsp water

Cold Dough

100 g/4 oz flour	50 ml/2 fl oz water
50 g/2 oz lard	

Filling

25 g/1 oz butter	350 g/12 oz cooked
25 g/1 oz flour	chicken
300 ml/½ pint milk	2-3 mushrooms
salt and pepper	(optional)
1 tbsp parsley	1 egg, beaten

The half puff pastry must be made first to allow it time to rest. Rub together the flour and lard to make rough crumbs. Add the water to make a dough. Knead well. Begin to roll out the dough. Cut the margarine into small pieces and dot over the dough. Gently fold the dough in thirds, turn so that the open edge faces you and roll again. Do not press down too hard. Fold again, turn so that the open edge faces you and roll. Fold once more and leave the dough to rest for at least 30 minutes.

Make the cold dough by rubbing the flour and lard together and binding with water.

Melt the butter for filling, stir in the flour and slowly add the milk. Cook, stirring constantly, until the sauce has thickened. Season with salt and pepper. Dice the chicken and mushrooms, if you are using them. Add to the sauce, along with the parsley, and stir well.

When you are assembling the pies, roll out the half puff pastry first. Cut rounds large enough to make lids for two 23-cm/9-inch pies. Leave to rest. Roll out the cold dough. Place the trimmings from the half puff pastry on top, fold and roll again. Line the two 23-cm/9-inch tins. Fill the pies and seal the lids with beaten egg. Use the remaining egg to glaze the top of the pies. Decorate with any trimmings or freeze any pastry which is left for use on another day. Bake the pies for 35 minutes at 190C/375F/gas 5 until they are golden.

This recipe works equally well with cooked turkey or lamb. If you are using lamb, flavour the sauce with 1 tbsp of mint sauce and omit the mushrooms. Other seasonings can also be added to the sauce, e.g. curry powder or herbs or a few cooked vegetables can be mixed in. *Each pie serves 4 people*

SWEENEY'S MEAT PIES

June and Alan use two kinds of pastry to prevent the bases of the pies getting soggy during baking. Instead, both crusts are light and flaky, with a lovely contrast in textures. Large quantities are given here to allow for variations – make one plain meat pie, and add either some mushrooms or smoked oysters or kidneys to others.

Half Puff Pastry

225 g/8 oz flour	75 g/3 oz margarine
40 g/1½ oz lard	100 ml/4 fl oz water

Cold Dough

175 g/6 oz flour	4½ tbsp water
75 g/3 oz lard	

Filling

450 g/1 lb beef, minced	2½ tbsp gravy powder
450 g/1 lb beef, cubed	2½ tbsp cornflour
water to cover	50 ml/2 fl oz water

To make the pastries and assemble the pies, follow the instructions for Sweeney's Chicken Pie.

To make the filling, combine the minced and cubed beef in a pan and cover with water. The cubed beef should be in small pieces, perhaps 1.5 cm/¾ inch each. Bring to the boil and simmer until the meat is cooked, 1-1½ hours.

Combine the gravy powder, cornflour and water. Add to the meat and cook, stirring constantly, until the gravy has thickened. Cool slightly before turning into the pie dishes. Arrange some sliced mushrooms, diced smoked oysters or diced, cooked kidneys on top of each pie before placing the lid on, if desired. Seal and brush the lids with beaten egg and bake 25 minutes at 200C/400F/gas 6 until the pastry is golden.

These quantities make enough for three 9-inch pies, **each of which will serve 4**

PORK AND APPLE PIE

Pork and apple always go well together, and this pie is no exception. The sauce is fairly rich, and pre-cooking the meat serves to remove its fat content.

225 g/8 oz pastry	salt and pepper
450 g/1 lb lean pork	pinch nutmeg
225 g/8 oz belly pork	2 apples, sliced
2-3 tbsp flour	1 tbsp flour
50 g/2 oz butter	1½ tbsp brown sugar
2 onions, chopped	25 g/1 oz butter
100 ml/4 fl oz beef stock	2-3 tbsp milk **OR**
100 ml/4 fl oz cider	1 egg, beaten

For the pastry, use shortcrust or Sweeney's combination of cold dough and half puff.

Roll out two-thirds of the pastry, and line a 23-cm/9-inch deep pie dish. Set aside the remaining pastry to make the lid.

Dice the meat into 1-cm/½-inch cubes. Dredge in flour. Melt 15 g/½ oz butter and toss the meat until it is well browned. Add the remaining butter and cook the onion until it is soft. Stir in the stock and cider. Season with salt, pepper and nutmeg. Simmer gently, covered, for 1 hour until the meat is tender. Cool slightly.

Turn the meat mixture into the pie dish. Arrange the apple slices on top. Combine the flour and brown sugar. Rub in the butter until coarse crumbs are formed. Sprinkle these over the apples. Place the pastry lid on top and seal well. Use any trimmings to decorate the top of the pie. Brush with milk or beaten egg. Bake 1 hour at 190C/375F/ gas 5. ***Serves 4-6***

COULIBIAC

Russian cooking abounds with savoury pies, but this is one of the best known. Although it is traditionally made with fresh salmon, tinned produces an excellent pie.

225 g/8 oz puff pastry
213-g/7½-oz tin salmon
50 g/2 oz rice
3 hardboiled eggs
1 onion, finely chopped
175 g/6 oz mushrooms, chopped

50 g/2 oz butter
1½ tbsp white wine
salt and pepper
1 tsp parsley
½ tsp dill seeds
1 egg, beaten

Melt the butter and gently fry the onions and mushrooms until they are soft. Add the white wine, dill, parsley and salt and pepper. Simmer gently until most of the liquid has evaporated, 5 minutes approximately. Set aside to cool.

Cook the rice and set aside to cool. Flake the salmon and chop the hardboiled eggs. Roll out the pastry to make a large rectangle, approximately 15 x 25 cm/6 x 10 inch.

To assemble the pie, spread the salmon in a wide column down the centre of the pastry. Place a layer of chopped egg on top, then a layer of rice and finally a layer of onions and mushrooms. Brush the edges of the pastry with beaten egg and fold over to make a neat parcel. Trim the edges and seal well with egg. Gently turn the pie, seam side down, onto a greased, flat baking tray. Brush the remaining egg over the surface of the pie. Use any pastry trimmings to decorate the top and brush once more with egg. Make a few holes with a skewer to allow the steam to escape. Bake 30-40 minutes at 220C/425F/gas 7. **Serves 6-8**

FISH PIE

A highly spiced mixture of fish, tomatoes and small macaroni makes a lovely alternative to the traditional white fish pie. The crispy top crust is a nice contrast to the filling, and a pastry base is proved superfluous.

100 g/4 oz pastry
450 g/1 lb cod or haddock
  fillets
100 ml/4 fl oz olive oil
2 cloves garlic, chopped
2 dried chillies, chopped
425-g/15-oz tin tomatoes,
  sieved

4 anchovy fillets
1 tbsp parsley
¼ tsp pepper
100 g/4 oz small
  macaroni
100 g/4 oz prawns
  (optional)

Skin the fish and cut into 2.5-cm/1-inch pieces. Chop the anchovies. Heat the olive oil. Gently cook the garlic, chillies and anchovies for 2 minutes, stirring to blend the flavours. Add the fish. Mix well, then stir in the tomatoes, parsley and pepper. Simmer until the fish is cooked, 15 minutes approximately.

Cook the macaroni until it is just beginning to soften. Drain well, rinse with cold water and drain again. Check the fish to correct the seasoning. Mix in the macaroni and prawns if you are using them. Cook 1 minute longer to blend the flavours. Turn into a 23-cm/9-in deep pie dish.

Roll out your favourite savoury pastry and make a lid over the fish mixture. Puff pastry, cheese pastry or shortcrust made with vegetable fat would all be suitable. Bake 20 minutes at 200C/400F/gas 6. ***Serves 4-6***

PISSALADIÈRE

A thick tomato and onion sauce is garnished with anchovies and black olives to make a delicious lunch or supper dish – simply add salad and crusty bread when serving.

175 g/6 oz pastry
3 onions, chopped
3 cloves garlic, chopped
50 ml/2 fl oz olive oil
425-g/15-oz tin tomatoes
2-3 tbsp tomato purée

1 tsp parsley
1 tsp basil
salt and pepper
pinch sugar
4-6 anchovy fillets
10-12 black olives

Heat the olive oil and slowly fry the onions and garlic until they are soft. Stir in the tomatoes, tomato purée, sugar and herbs. Simmer gently until the tomatoes have softened and the sauce is very thick – most of the liquid should evaporate. Season with pepper and a pinch of salt.

For the pastry, use shortcrust made with vegetable fat or half fat and half margarine. Roll out the pastry to fit a shallow 25-cm/10-inch pie or flan dish. Bake blind. Leave to cool.

Pour the sauce into the pastry case. Arrange the anchovy fillets and black olives over the top to garnish. Bake 15 minutes at 180C/350F/gas 4. ***Serves 4-6***

MIXED PEPPER TART

175 g/6 oz pastry	1½ tbsp olive oil
2 cloves garlic	½ tsp salt
1 large onion	250 ml/8 fl oz double cream
1 green pepper	2 eggs
1 red pepper	1 egg yolk
1 yellow pepper	1 tsp oregano

For the pastry, use a savoury shortcrust, flavoured with mustard or Parmesan cheese if you like it. Roll the pastry to fit a 23-cm/9-inch flan dish. Bake blind and allow to cool slightly.

Thinly slice the garlic, onion and peppers. If yellow peppers are difficult to obtain, use equal quantities of red and green. Heat the olive oil and gently sauté the vegetables until they are soft. Season with salt and oregano.

Beat the eggs and yolk with the double cream. Add the vegetables and mix well. Turn into the pastry case. Bake 30-35 minutes at 190C/375F/gas 5 or until set. Slices of tomato can be added as a garnish 15 minutes after the pie has been placed in the oven. *Serves 4-6*

COURGETTE TART

Although there is quite a lot of preparation involved in the making of this tart, it is definitely a case of the end justifying the means. The sauce is light and well flavoured to enhance the delicate courgettes. It would be equally well suited to a buffet, lunch or as a starter for a special meal.

175 g/6 oz flour
1 tbsp Parmesan cheese
½ tsp dry mustard
½ tsp paprika
75 g/3 oz butter
2-3 tbsp cold water
450 g/1 lb courgettes
50 g/2 oz butter
1 clove garlic

juice and rind of ½ lemon
salt and pepper
25 g/1 oz butter
3 tbsp flour
150 ml/¼ pint milk
150 ml/¼ pint soured
    cream
1 egg, separated
175 g/6 oz Cheddar, grated

Combine 175 g/6 oz flour with Parmesan, mustard and paprika. Rub in 75 g/3 oz of butter to make fine crumbs. Add enough water to bind into a firm dough. Roll out and line a 23-cm/9-inch shallow pie dish. Bake bind. Allow to cool slightly.

Melt 50 g/2 oz butter. Sauté the thinly sliced courgettes with chopped garlic, grated lemon rind and lemon juice until they are golden. Season with salt and pepper. Drain well, reserving the liquid, and set aside to cool.

Add 25 g/1 oz of butter to the liquid left from the courgettes. Stir in 3 tbsp flour. Slowly add the milk and cook, stirring constantly, until the sauce is thick. Remove from the heat. Stir in the soured cream, egg yolk and grated cheese. Beat the egg white until it is stiff, but not dry. Gently fold it into the sauce. Pour the sauce into the pastry case. Arrange the courgettes over the surface of the tart. Bake 15 minutes at 180C/350F/gas 4. Remove from the oven and allow to cool for 10 minutes before serving – just enough to let the filling set slightly. ***Serves 4-6***

CHEESE AND POTATO PIE

A hearty supper dish which needs little accompaniment – perhaps a green vegetable or some sausages. Although potatoes and pastry may seem stodgy, they are far from that in this lightly flavoured pie.

225 g/8 oz puff pastry	1 tbsp parsley
450 g/1 lb potatoes	salt and pepper
75 g/3 oz Gruyère cheese, grated	50 g/2 oz butter
1 medium onion, chopped	1 egg, beaten
2 cloves garlic, chopped	2 tbsp top of the milk
	100 ml/4 fl oz double cream

Roll out three-quarters of the pastry to fit into the base and sides of an 18-cm/7-inch cake tin. Set aside the trimmings to make the lid of the pie.

Peel the potatoes and slice them as thinly as possible. Blanch in boiling water for 2 minutes. Drain and allow to cool slightly.

Mix 2 tbsp of double cream with the egg. Mix the remaining cream with 2 tbsp top of the milk.

To assemble the pie, place a layer of potatoes in the pastry case. Top with chopped onions and garlic. Season with parsley, salt and pepper. Sprinkle on the grated cheese. Repeat until all the filling ingredients have been used. Very carefully pour the cream and milk mixture over the pie. If there is too much, save the remainder and slowly pour it into the pie 10 minutes before cooking is complete through a vent made in the top crust.

Make a lid from the pastry. Seal it on and glaze with the egg and cream mixture. Make a hole in the lid to allow steam to escape. Bake 45 minutes at 200C/400F/gas 6, brushing once again with egg and cream halfway through the cooking time. **Serves 4-6**

Pizza is yet another of the foods which have very loose guidelines and infinite variations. The yeast dough given below is closer to the authentic Italian pizza, but the quick dough is delicious and an easy substitute. Tomato sauce and cheese are a must but the other toppings are according to taste. In any case, pizza freezes well and makes excellent snacks, lunches or suppers, especially when served with a green salad.

Yeast Dough

1 tsp dry yeast	1 tsp salt
½ tsp sugar	225 g/8 oz plain flour
150 ml/¼ pint warm water	1 tbsp olive oil

Quick Dough

225 g/8 oz plain flour	75 g/3 oz margarine
3 tsp baking powder	100-150 ml/4 fl oz-¼ pint
1 tsp salt	milk

Tomato Sauce

425-g/15-oz tin tomatoes, sieved	1 tbsp oregano
1 clove garlic, sliced	2 tbsp olive oil
1 tbsp basil OR	pinch sugar
	¼ tsp salt

Toppings

75 g/3 oz Mozzarella or Gruyère cheese	1-2 tbsp olive oil
2 tbsp Parmesan cheese	mushrooms, peppers,
1 small onion, chopped	salami, anchovies, olives
	etc. to taste

To make the yeast dough, dissolve the sugar and dry yeast in the warm water. Leave for 10 minutes until the yeast is bubbly. Gradually add to the combined flour, salt and olive oil to make a stiff dough. Knead until it is smooth. Place the dough in a clean bowl, cover with a cloth or wrap in a plastic bag. Leave it in a warm place until it is doubled in bulk, 1-2 hours. To test, poke a finger gently into the dough. If the hole remains, the dough has risen sufficiently. Roll out as thinly as possible – make two pizzas if necessary – and place on a flat baking tray or on the base of a shallow flan dish. Remember that the dough will rise somewhat during baking.

To make the quick dough, combine the dry ingredients. Rub in the margarine until soft crumbs have formed, then slowly add the milk to form a stiff dough. Knead until it is smooth. Roll out as thinly as possible – make two pizzas if necessary – and place on a flat baking tray or on the base of a shallow flan dish. This dough will rise considerably during baking.

For the sauce, heat the olive oil and quickly fry the garlic until it is golden. Add the tomatoes and seasoning. Simmer gently for 20 minutes.

Spread the sauce over the dough. Gently fry the onion in olive oil until it is soft. Spread over the sauce. Sprinkle on the grated Mozzarella or Gruyère. If you are using any other toppings, e.g. sautéed mushrooms, peppers, sliced salami, olives, anchovies, etc. arrange these over the cheese. Cover with Parmesan. Bake 15-20 minutes at 220C/425F/gas 7.
Serves 4-6

QUICHES

Savoury quiches are versatile and popular. The varieties are endless. Using 100g/4 oz of pastry and a 23-cm/9-in pie dish, any of the following basic fillings can be used, enhanced by the garnishes which follow, or anything else which may come to mind. Always bake the pastry case first to prevent it becoming soggy, but thereafter, let your imagination be your guide.

WHITE SAUCE

2 tbsp butter
2 tbsp flour
salt and pepper
150 ml/¼ pint milk **OR**

250 ml/8 fl oz single cream
OR
150 ml/¼ pint stock

Melt the butter and stir in the flour. Cook for 1 minute. Slowly add the liquid. Cook, stirring constantly, until the sauce is thickened. Season with salt and pepper.

LIGHT CUSTARD

2 eggs
150 ml/¼ pint milk

2 tbsp single cream
salt and pepper

Beat the eggs, stir in the cream and season with salt and pepper.

RICH CUSTARD

2 eggs
1 egg yolk
salt and pepper

300 ml/½ pint cream
(single or double, to
taste)

Beat the eggs, stir in the milk and cream and season.

CHEESE CUSTARD

225 g/8 oz cream cheese
3 eggs

150 ml/¼ pint milk
salt and pepper

Beat the cream cheese until it is light and fluffy. Beat in the eggs, one at a time, and then the milk. Season.

Garnishes should be prepared separately and can then be folded into the basic filling mixture, or arranged at the bottom of the pastry case with the filling poured over; otherwise the filling can be poured in first, baked for 10 minutes to begin setting it and then the garnish can be arranged on top.

2 thinly sliced onions, fried in 50g/2 oz butter, seasoned with paprika.

Thinly sliced leeks, mushrooms, peppers etc. sautéed in butter.

Chopped spinach, cooked and seasoned.

Crisply fried, diced bacon.

Mixed herbs – fresh or dried.

Seafood mixed with spring onions or chives, seasoned with cayenne.

Cream cheese mixed with dates, nuts or smoked salmon.

Any variety of grated cheese, particularly Gruyère or Cheddar.

Salami, smoked sausage or ham.

CHOCOLATE CREAM PIE

A sweet but light pie which can make a lovely finish for a dinner party. It is also a great favourite with the children. The biscuits for the base can be digestive, morning coffee, rich tea or ginger snaps.

Base

75 g/3 oz biscuit crumbs	50 g/2 oz butter, melted
2 tbsp sugar	

Filling

50 g/2 oz sugar	1 egg, separated
25 g/1 oz flour	1 tbsp butter
2 tbsp cocoa	1 tsp vanilla **OR**
pinch salt	1 tbsp brandy **OR**
250 ml/8 fl oz milk	1 tbsp rum

To make the biscuit base, combine the crumbs and sugar and stir in the melted butter thoroughly to moisten the mixture. Turn into a 20-cm/8-inch flan dish and press down gently over the base and 5mm/¼ inch up the sides of the dish. Chill while you prepare the filling.

Mix together the sugar, flour, cocoa and salt. Add enough milk to make a thick paste. Heat the remaining milk until it is just boiling. Slowly add the hot milk to the paste, stirring constantly. Return the filling mixture to the pan and stir over a low heat until it has thickened. Remove from the heat and mix in the egg yolk; vanilla, or brandy, or rum and butter. Allow to cool slightly. Cover with grease-proof paper to prevent a skin forming.

Beat the egg white until it is stiff but not dry. Gently fold into the cooled chocolate mixture. Pour the filling over the crumb base and chill for 2-3 hours before serving. The pie can be garnished with whipped cream, chopped nuts, glacé cherries or chocolate flakes to make it more attractive.
Serves 6

BLACK CHERRY TART

Black cherries blend particularly well with rum and the contrast of smooth custard with chunks of fruit produces a lovely finish to a special meal.

225 g/8 oz pâte sucrée
225 g/8 oz black cherries
2 tbsp morello jam
2 eggs, beaten
50 g/2 oz sugar

50 g/2 oz flour
2 tbsp rum
50 g/2 oz butter, melted
150 ml/¼ pint milk

Roll out the pâte sucrée to fit a 23-cm/9-inch flan dish. Spread the jam over the pastry base.

Drain the cherries and stone them. Combine the sugar and flour. Stir in the eggs, Gently stir in the rum, butter and milk. Add the cherries and pour the mixture onto the pastry base. Bake 30-40 minutes at 180C/350F/gas 4. ***Serves 5-6***

LEMON SOUFFLÉ TART

There are two ways of making the lemon filling for this tart, depending on the amount of time you have to spend on it. The short cut method, using lemon pie filling, is just as successful as the home made version.

50g/2 oz afternoon tea or digestive biscuits

40 g/1½ oz butter, melted

Filling 1

1 package lemon pie filling

1 egg yolk

300 ml/½ pint water

2 egg whites

½ tbsp sugar

Filling 2

1 lemon

2 eggs, separated

175 g/6 oz sugar

1 heaped tbsp cornflour

450 ml/¾ pint water

For the pie crust, crush the biscuits into fine crumbs and combine with the melted butter. Press on to the base, and slightly up the sides of a 20-cm/8-inch pie dish. Chill until the filling is ready.

For Filling 1, combine the pie filling with the egg yolk and water. Cook, stirring constantly, until the mixture has come to the boil and the lemon flavoured capsule has burst. Cool slightly. Beat the egg whites with the sugar until they are stiff, but not dry. Gently fold into the lemon mixture. Turn into the pie dish and chill until set.

For Filling 2, grate the rind of the lemon and squeeze the juice. Combine the sugar and cornflour. Slowly add the egg yolks, water, lemon juice and rind. Cook, stirring constantly, until the mixture thickens and comes to the boil. Simmer gently for 5 minutes. Cool slightly. Beat the egg whites until they are stiff, but not dry. Gently fold into the lemon mixture. Turn into the pie dish and chill until set.

If desired, the pie can be garnished with whipped cream, or pouring cream can be served separately. ***Serves 5-6***

MERINGUE FRUIT PIE

Lemons are not the only fruit which combine well with meringue. Fresh, tinned or dried fruit can be used, and dressing the pastry and meringue up with some ground nuts adds a dimension which will make a hit every time.

175 g/6 oz pastry

Meringue

2 egg whites	**1 tbsp sugar**
2 tbsp ground almonds	

Filling

350 g/12 oz fruit	**2 tbsp sugar**
juice and rind of ½ lemon	**2 egg yolks**

For the pastry, use shortcrust, enhanced with ground almonds if desired, or any other sweet pastry. Roll out and line a 23-cm/9-inch pie dish. Bake blind until the pastry is crisp and golden. Set aside to cool.

If dried fruit is being used, this should be left to soak overnight. To dress up the pie further, the fruit can be soaked in kirsch. When you are ready to prepare the filling, gently cook the fruit in a covered pan with the sugar and lemon juice and rind until it is a thick pulp. Remove from the heat and stir in the egg yolks. Turn into the pastry case and bake until it is set, approximately 20 minutes at 180C/350F/gas 4.

Beat the egg whites until they are stiff but not dry. Very gently fold in the sugar and almonds. Arrange the meringue over the fruit mixture and return to the oven for 5-10 minutes at 200C/400F/gas 6. Cool and chill before serving. Alternatively, fold the meringue into the pulped fruit and bake 30 minutes at 190C/375F/gas 5. ***Serves 6***

FRENCH FRUIT PIE

French bakeries offer such a delicious range of pastries that making a choice is half the fun. The delicate crème patissière which is used must be an all time favourite. Strawberries are the traditional fruit, but plums, greengages, cherries etc. can also be used.

350 g/12 oz pâte sucrée	225 g/8 oz fruit

Crème Patissière

1 egg	15 g/½ oz cornflour
1 egg yolk	20 g/¾ oz flour
50 g/2 oz sugar	300 ml/½ pint milk

Glaze

3 tbsp apricot jam OR	1 tsp lemon juice
3 tbsp redcurrant jelly	1 tbsp water

Roll out the pâte sucrée to line a 23-cm/9-inch pie dish or 12 individual pie dishes. Bake 10-20 minutes at 190C/375F/ gas 5 until the pastry is golden. Set aside to cool.

To prepare the crème patissière, combine the sugar, cornflour and flour. Mix in the egg and extra yolk. Add enough milk to make a thick paste. Heat the remaining milk until it just reaches boiling point. Slowly stir the hot milk into the paste. Return to the pan and heat, stirring constantly, until the mixture thickens. Allow to cool, then spoon into the pastry case. Arange the fruit on top.

To prepare the glaze, heat the apricot jam (if you are using greengages) or redcurrant jelly (if you are using strawber- ries, plums or cherries) with the lemon juice and water until it reaches boiling point. Simmer gently for 5 minutes until it is thick and smooth. Brush the glaze over the pies and leave to set. These pies are best served on the day they are made, as they tend to get soggy if left overnight. ***Serves 12***

FRUIT CRUMB PIE

*Fruit pies are always popular and the recipe here offers an
alternative to the double-crusted variety. The pastry is
particularly soft and crumbly, and the topping of coarse crumbs
sets off the filling beautifully. The best fruits to use are cherries,
plums, greengages or apples, although other fruits can also be
successful.*

Pastry

175 g/6 oz flour
¾ tsp baking powder
pinch salt
2 tbsp sugar

1 egg, beaten
100 g/4 oz butter
1 tbsp milk

Filling

275-350 g/10-12 oz fruit
50 g/2 oz sugar
1 tsp cornflour

½ tsp cinnamon
2 tbsp water

Topping

50 g/2 oz flour
1 tbsp sugar

25 g/1 oz butter
1 tsp cinnamon (optional)

To make the pastry, combine all the dry ingredients. Rub in
the butter to make coarse crumbs and bind the pastry with
the egg and milk. Gently press the dough into a 23-cm/9-
inch tin covering the base and sides.

Combine the cornflour, cinnamon and sugar for the
filling. Add the fruit and mix well. Stir in the water. Turn
into the pastry case.

To make the topping, rub together the flour, sugar and
butter to make coarse crumbs. Sprinkle over the fruit filling.
Bake for 40 minutes at 200C/400F/gas 6 or until the pastry is
golden. Serve warm or cold. ***Serves 8***

*Apples are so versatile that an entire book could be devoted to
them. Falling short of that, the recipes included here offer simple
but elegant choices. They are both open pies, and should offer
new ideas to add to old favourites.*

175 g/6 oz pastry
350 g/12 oz apple purée
2 apples, thinly sliced
1 tbsp sugar

2 tbsp apricot jam OR
2 tbsp marmalade
2 tbsp water

For the pastry, use pâte sucrée, shortcrust or your favourite
sweet pastry. Roll out thinly and line a 23-cm/9-inch pie
dish.

Fill the pastry case with the apple purée. Arrange the
apple slices carefully on top and sprinkle with sugar. Bake
25 minutes at 180C/350F/gas 4 until the apple slices are
golden.

Combine the jam or marmalade with water and heat
gently until the mixture is thick and smooth. Brush the glaze
carefully over the top of the pie. Serve warm or cold. **Serves
4-6**

APPLE PIE (2)

The apples in this pie retain some of their crispness to contrast with the soft custard and pastry.

175 g/6 oz pastry	**1 egg**
2 apples, thinly sliced	**½ tsp vanilla**
2 tbsp sugar	**150 ml/¼ pint milk**
1 tbsp flour	**2 tbsp icing sugar**

For the pastry, use a shortcrust made with butter only, or any other soft, sweet pastry. Roll out and line a 23-cm/9-inch pie dish.

Arrange the thinly sliced apples over the pastry base. Sprinkle with 1 tbsp of sugar. Bake 15 minutes at 160C/325F/gas 3 until the apples are just beginning to soften.

Combine the flour and remaining 1 tbsp of sugar. Stir in the egg, vanilla and milk. Carefully pour this mixture over the apples and bake 20 minutes longer at 180C/350F/gas 4 or until the custard is set. Cool slightly, then sprinkle with icing sugar. Serve warm or cold. ***Serves 4-6***

PUMPKIN PIE

Always associated with America and Thanksgiving, this pie is rarely seen elsewhere. It is, however, a treat which does not deserve to be so sadly neglected. The texture is smooth, as with a custard pie, and the flavour slightly spicy.

175 g/6 oz pastry	225 g/8 oz sugar
425-g/15-oz tin pumpkin	1 tsp cinnamon
397-g/14-oz tin evaporated milk	½ tsp each ground cloves, ginger, nutmeg, salt and
2 eggs, beaten	mixed spice

Combine the sugar and spices. Beat together the pumpkin and eggs. Add the sugar mixture and beat well. Slowly stir in the evaporated milk.

For the pastry, use a sweet shortcrust made with sugar and egg yolk or a soft margarine. Roll out the pastry to fill a 24-cm/9½-inch deep pie dish. Place the dish on a baking tray in case the pumpkin mixture overflows slightly during baking. Pour the filling into the pastry shell. Bake 15 minutes at 220C/425F/gas 7 then reduce the heat to 180C/350F/gas 4 for an additional 50-60 minutes, or until the filling has set. Chill and serve with cream on the side or garnished with whipped cream. ***Serves 8-10***